CUTAWAY
RACING CARS

JON RICHARDS

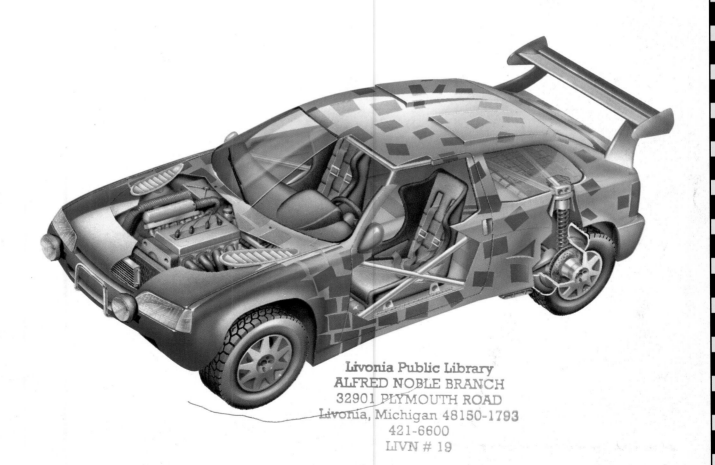

COPPER BEECH BOOKS
BROOKFIELD, CONNECTICUT

© Aladdin Books Ltd 1998
© U.S. text 1998

Designed and produced by
Aladdin Books Ltd
28 Percy Street
London W1P 0LD

First published in the United States in 1998 by
Copper Beech Books,
an imprint of
The Millbrook Press
2 Old New Milford Road
Brookfield, Connecticut
06804

Editor
Sarah Levete
Consultant
Steve Allman
Design
David West
Children's Book Design
Designer
Robert Perry
Illustrators
Simon Tegg & Ross Watton
Picture Research
Brooks Krikler Research

CIP data is on file at the
Library of Congress.

ISBN 0-7613-0727-3 (trade)
ISBN 0-7613-0720-6 (lib. bdg.)

CONTENTS

INTRODUCTION

Motor racing is very exciting. Cars zoom around racetracks at high speeds, trying to finish the course in the shortest possible time. There are many different types of racing cars in different parts of the world. They can be simple and small, like go-karts, or powerful and packed full of high-tech equipment, like Formula One racing cars.

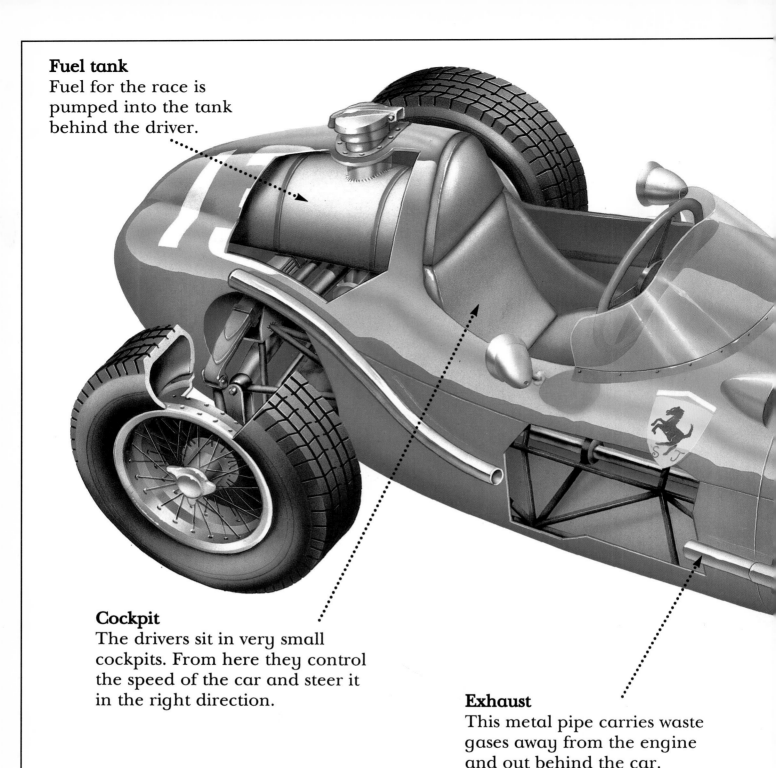

Fuel tank
Fuel for the race is
pumped into the tank
behind the driver.

Cockpit
The drivers sit in very small
cockpits. From here they control
the speed of the car and steer it
in the right direction.

Exhaust
This metal pipe carries waste
gases away from the engine
and out behind the car.

OLD RACER

This car raced in Grand Prix during the
late 1950s. Even then, racing cars looked
very different from normal road cars.

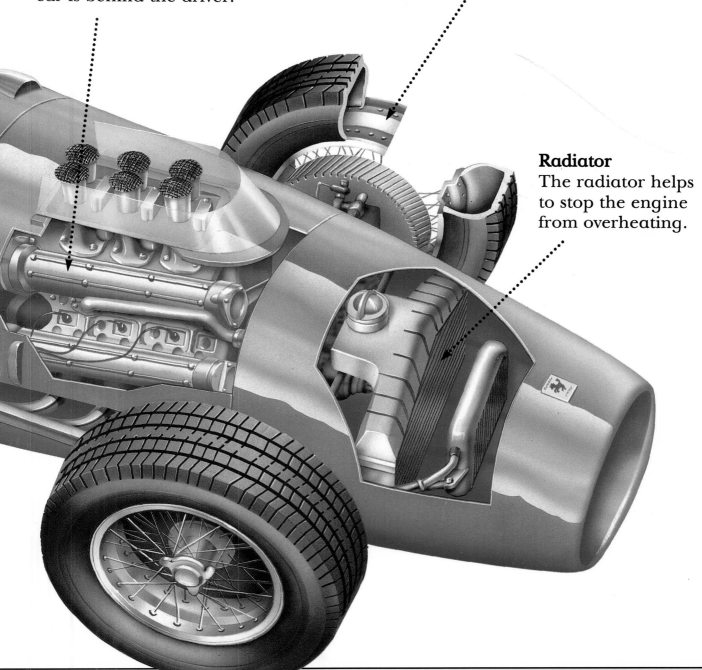

Engine
The engine for this old racing car sits in front of the driver. Today, the engine in a Formula One car is behind the driver.

Wheels
Unlike modern racing wheels, these wheels have wire spokes. They are also much thinner than modern racing wheels.

Radiator
The radiator helps to stop the engine from overheating.

They had much more powerful engines, specially built bodies to help them go faster, and their drivers sat in small cockpits.

However, these old front-engined cars were replaced by cars with their engines placed behind the driver.

Racing has changed

Modern racing cars

This 1970s Formula One car (*right*) is very similar to today's racing vehicles. Its engine is behind the driver, it has fat tires to help it grip the track, and it has large "wings" to help the car drive faster (*see* page 8).

Cockpit

Rear wing

Rear wheel

Changing shapes

Over the years, designers and mechanics have looked at ways of making the cars move through the air more easily. As a result, today's cars are more streamlined than the bulkier shapes of the earliest racers (*left*).

a lot over the years.

Strange racing cars

People who build racing cars have tried many ways to make their cars go faster. These have included making the engines very powerful and even building a car that had six wheels (*right*).

Nose

Six-wheeled racing car

Running start

Some races used to begin with the drivers running to their cars across the track (*right*). However, this has now been stopped because it became dangerous for the drivers.

Wings

As air flows over these "wings," it pushes the car down onto the track. This helps the tires to grip, stopping them from slipping. This allows the car to go faster (*see* page 19).

Roll bar

The roll bar is found just behind the driver's head. It protects the driver if the car turns over.

Cockpit

The driver sits in a cockpit made from a tough material called carbon fiber. This protects the driver in a crash.

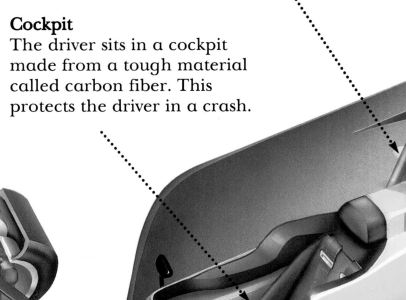

INDY CAR

This type of racer is called an Indy car. It has a specially designed body, with fins and wings, and a very powerful engine. These mean that the Indy car can zoom around tracks at speeds of over 200 mph (320 km/h) — that's more than twice as fast as a normal road car!

Indy cars are often raced around oval-shaped tracks. The oval tracks have banked corners that are raised on the outside. These let the cars go even faster!

Tires
An Indy car can use two types of tires. One is fitted in dry weather. It is called a "slick." The other type is fitted in wet weather. It has a deep pattern on its surface to help the car drive in the rain.

There are many ways

Tire walls

Some parts of a racetrack are lined with walls made from stacks of old tires (*above*). These provide a springy barrier to stop cars if they crash into them.

Gravel traps

Around other parts of a racetrack there may be large areas covered with gravel. When a car comes off the track, the gravel slows the car down, gradually and safely (*above*).

to keep a race safe.

Tough on the track

Because racing cars are traveling very quickly, any crashes that occur can be dangerous (*above*). To protect the drivers, parts of the cars are made from very strong materials, such as carbon fiber (*see* page 8).

The pace car

After a bad crash, a pace car is sent onto the track. The racing cars have to slow down and line up behind the pace car (*right*) until the wreckage has been cleared.

Engine
This must be very powerful to drive the car quickly. It must also run for a very long time without developing any faults.

Driving seat
The driver is held securely in place by a specially shaped seat and a strong harness.

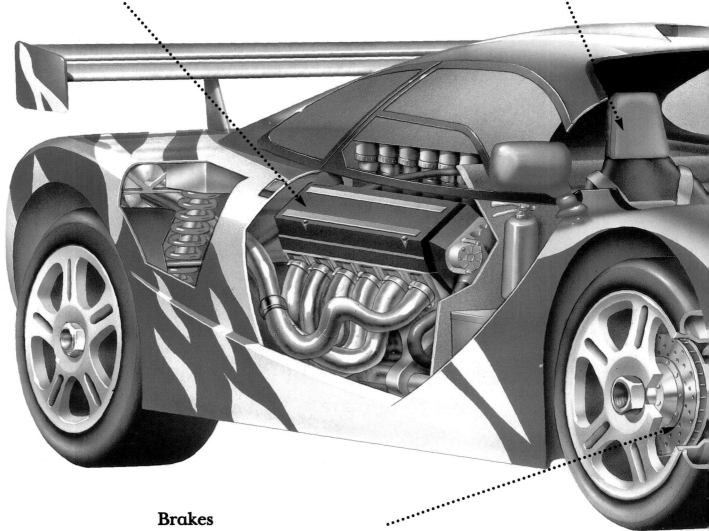

Brakes
During a race, the brakes of a racing car get very hot as they are used to slow the car — sometimes they can glow with the heat!

ENDURANCE RACER
Many races can go on for a very long time — some of them can last for 24 hours! They are called endurance races.

Windshield
The windshield of an endurance racer is very large. This gives the driver as clear a view of the road as possible.

Wing mirrors
These special mirrors on the side of the car help the drivers to see behind them.

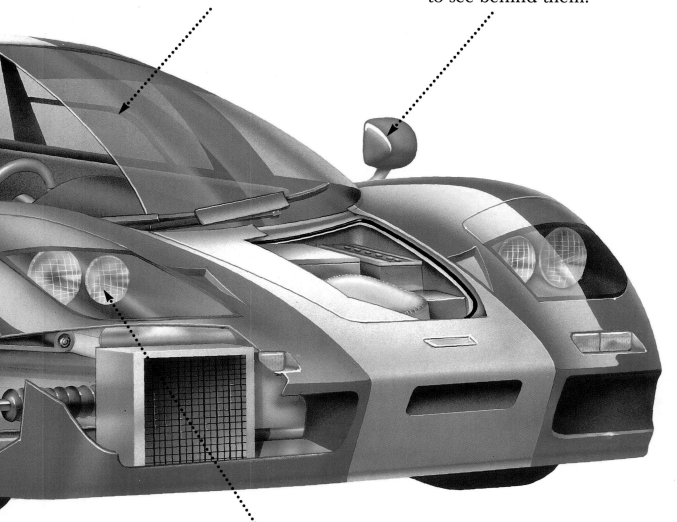

Headlights
During a 24-hour race the cars have to drive through the night. To help the drivers see, the cars have bright headlights.

During these races, teams of two or three drivers take turns to drive the car as far as possible within the time limit.

When the car pulls into the pits (*see* pages 20-21) one driver leaps out of the car and another gets in to continue the race.

Race teams have lots

A race team

The drivers are only a small part of the entire race team (*right*). Behind them are the team managers, engineers, mechanics, and technicians who work on the cars at each race. Then, at the team headquarters, there are designers and builders. They work on the racing car's design and try to improve its performance.

New designs

Designers and builders use the latest technology to create faster cars (*left*). They can see how these new models will perform by testing them using wind tunnels and computers.

# of people in them.

Team trucks

Massive trucks (*above*) are used to carry the team's equipment. Inside them is everything the team needs, including the cars, spare tires, and even spare engines.

Mechanics

A number of mechanics travel with the team's cars. They fit engines into each of the cars and adjust other parts of the cars to suit the conditions for each race (*right*).

What it takes to

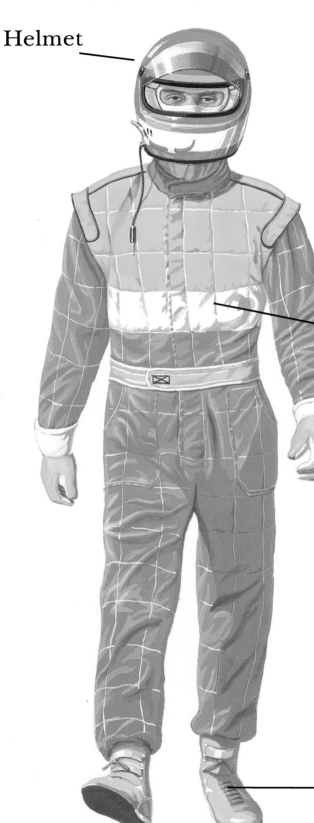

Helmet

Helmets

To protect their heads, drivers wear helmets made from a tough material called fiber glass. The helmets have a tube through which the drivers can drink. There is also a radio to keep them in touch with the pits.

Driving suit

Gloves

Body protection

The driving suit, gloves, and boots are made from fireproof materials. Beneath these may be another layer of fireproof underclothes, including a balaclava that covers the head and face.

Boots

be a racing driver.

Training

Driving a racing car during a long race is very tiring. To stay fit drivers have to watch what they eat and get regular exercise (*right*).

In the cockpit

In some racing cars the drivers have to squeeze into a tight cockpit where there is little room to move (*left*). In front of them are the instruments and the steering wheel.

Examining figures

The car is fitted with sensors that record what the drivers do. These figures are sent back to the pits by radio. The drivers and mechanics can then look at these figures to see how the car can be driven faster (*right*).

RALLY CAR

Not all racing cars are driven on roads. Rally cars race each other over almost any kind of ground, from dirt tracks to snow, and even through large deserts! These cars have to be specially altered so that they can cope with very rough ground.

Inside the rally car, a codriver sits next to the driver. He tells the driver what corners or obstacles are coming next along the track. The driver can then set the speed and direction of the car to match the course.

Air vents
These special holes in the top of the hood, called vents, help to keep the engine cool.

Engine
The powerful engine in this racing car is in front of the driver.

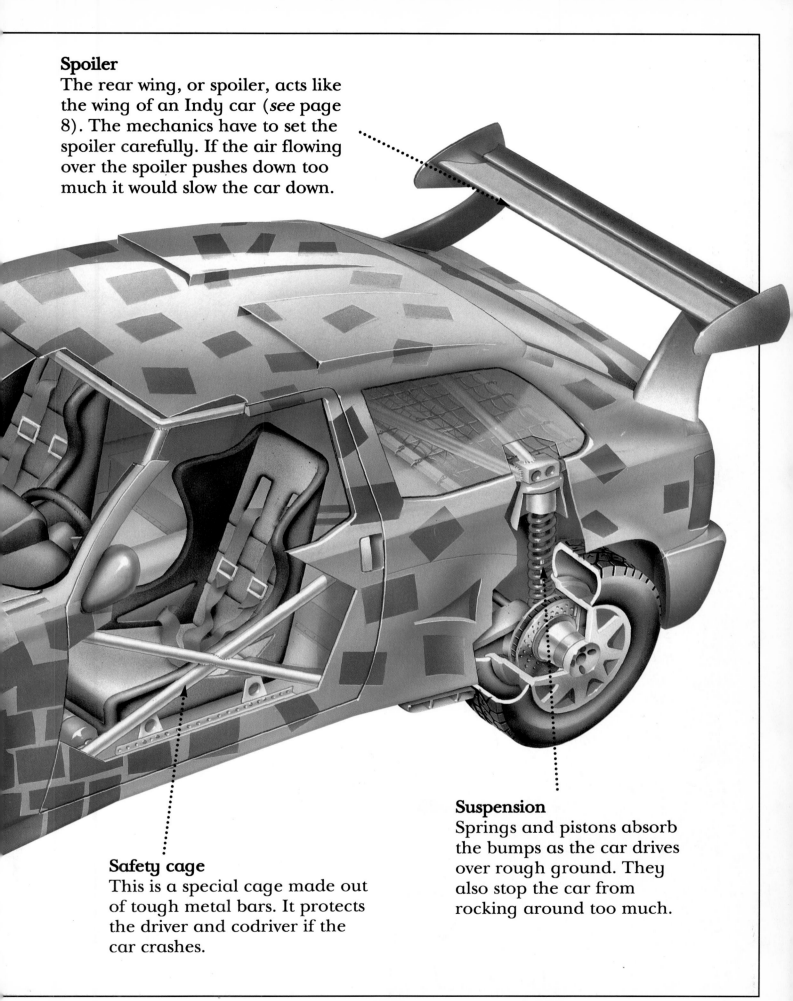

Spoiler
The rear wing, or spoiler, acts like the wing of an Indy car (*see* page 8). The mechanics have to set the spoiler carefully. If the air flowing over the spoiler pushes down too much it would slow the car down.

Safety cage
This is a special cage made out of tough metal bars. It protects the driver and codriver if the car crashes.

Suspension
Springs and pistons absorb the bumps as the car drives over rough ground. They also stop the car from rocking around too much.

19

Sometimes a car has

The pits
Cars may pull into the pits during a race. These are places where the mechanics can work on the car (*right*). They may need to change tires, add more fuel, swap drivers, or replace a broken part.

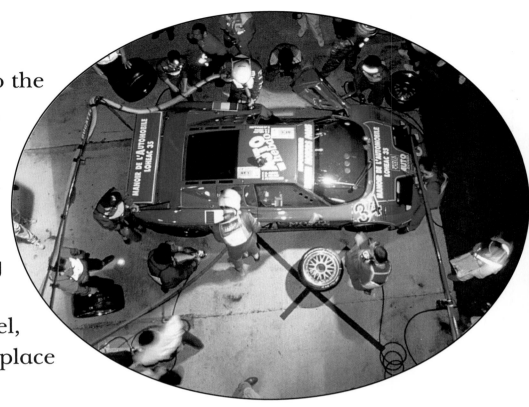

Fill the tank
Racing cars use up a lot of fuel. When they come into the pits, an exact amount of fuel is pumped into the fuel tank (*left*). This fuel lets the car finish the next part of the race.

to pull into the pits.

Pit safety

Because there is a lot of fuel around the pits, accidents can sometimes occur (*above*). Mechanics have to wear fireproof suits just like the drivers (*see* page 16).

Nighttime pits

During endurance races, mechanics in the pits need to be alert throughout the whole event. A pit stop could occur at any time — even in the middle of the night (*right*)!

Fuel tank
In a single race a dragster will use up enough fuel to fill a bathtub!

Body shape
The dragster is pointed at the front and is fitted with huge wings to help it slice through the air as quickly as possible.

Tires
Dragsters have huge fat tires at the back and very thin tires at the front.

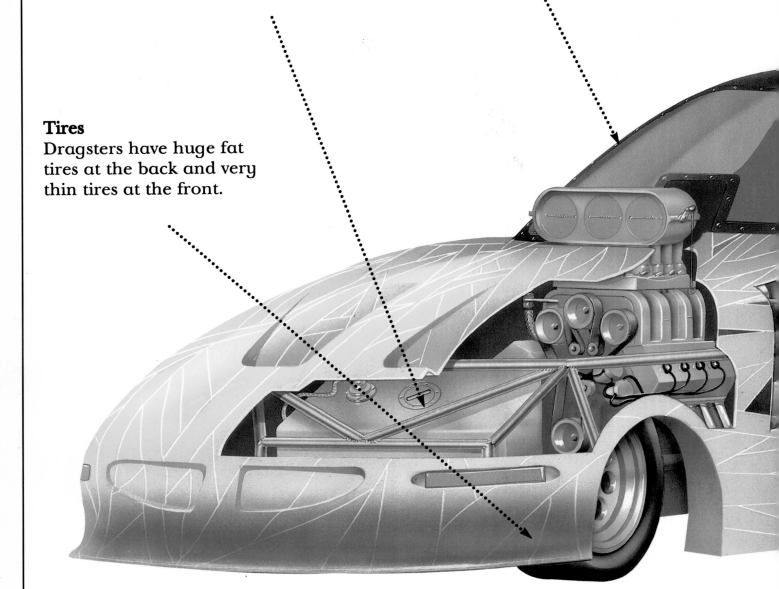

DRAGSTER
Dragsters are specially built cars that are designed for one thing — racing as quickly as possible along a straight track.

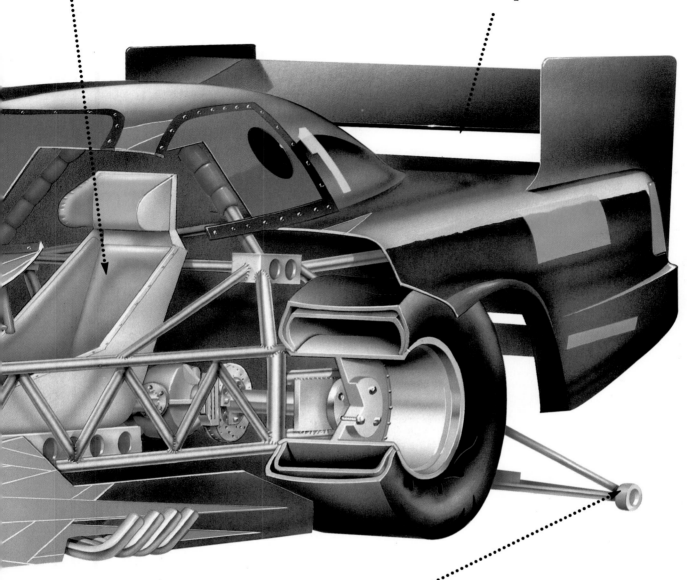

Cockpit
Inside the dragster is a safety cage similar to one in a rally car (*see* page 19). The cockpit is also fitted with a fire extinguisher.

Parachute
At the back of a dragster is a parachute. At the end of a race the driver releases this to help slow the car down.

Wheelie bar
This special bar at the back stops the dragster from flipping over when it zooms off.

Before they start, the drivers will spin their wheels. This "burning rubber" helps the tires to grip. When the signal is given, they whiz off down the track to see who can cross the finish line in the quickest time. Races can last as little as five seconds!

Many events happen

On the grid

A qualifying session is held before a race. During this session, drivers race to decide their position on the starting lineup, called the grid (*left*). The fastest driver starts at the front of the grid, called pole position.

Overtaking

During the race, cars compete to take the lead. To do this a driver must overtake (*below*) all the other cars. Getting to the front requires a lot of skill.

during the race.

The finish

The winner of the race is the first past the finish line when all the laps have been driven. When the winner crosses the line a race official waves a black-and-white checkered flag (*right*).

On the podium

The winner of the race goes onto the podium, as well as the drivers who finished second and third. Here they receive their trophies and sometimes spray fountains of champagne over each other (*left*).

Spoiler
Mechanics adjust the stock car's spoiler (*see* page 19) before each race to give the best performance.

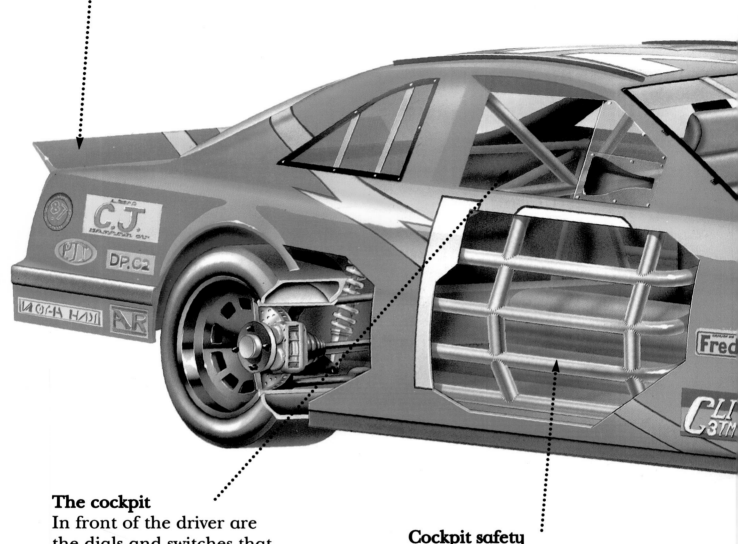

The cockpit
In front of the driver are the dials and switches that help the driver control the car and show how the car is performing.

Cockpit safety
The cockpit is surrounded by a strong safety cage made of metal bars. It is also fitted with a firefighting system.

STOCK CAR

These powerful machines are old road cars that have been converted into racing cars. Most of the time they race around oval

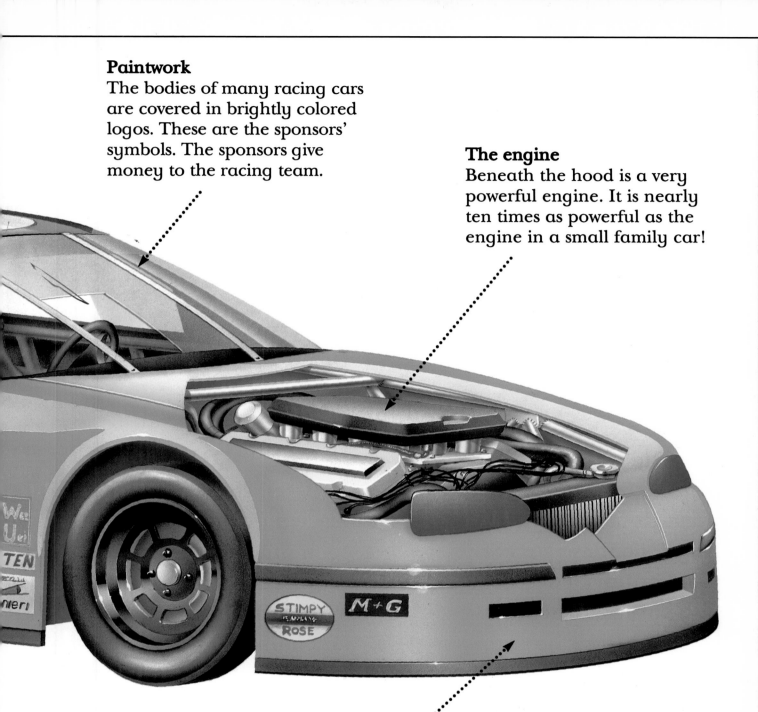

Paintwork
The bodies of many racing cars are covered in brightly colored logos. These are the sponsors' symbols. The sponsors give money to the racing team.

The engine
Beneath the hood is a very powerful engine. It is nearly ten times as powerful as the engine in a small family car!

Skirting
The front of the car is fitted with an extra piece of body kit, called a skirt. This skirt stops air from flowing under the car. If air did get under the car it would slow the car down.

courses like Indy cars (*see* pages 8-9). The cars may be bunched together at very high speed for the whole race. The slightest nudge can result in a spectacular crash! Because of this each car is built to protect the driver from any serious harm.

There are lots of

Hot rods

Put a powerful engine in an old car, paint it brightly, and you have a Hot Rod (*above*). Like dragsters, these cars are raced against each other on a straight track.

Dune buggies

In desert countries, lightweight cars called buggies race each other over sand dunes (*below*). These cars are little more than a safety cage and an engine on four wheels!

other racing cars.

Old timers

Very old cars (some nearly 100 years old) are still raced in many parts of the world (*right*). With these cars it is not so much winning the race as completing the course in one piece!

Go-karts

Although these racing cars are very small, they can still drive very quickly (*left*). Many of today's top racing drivers began their careers by racing go-karts.

Fantastic facts

• The first Grand Prix race was held at Le Mans in France in 1906. It was won by the French driver, Ferenc Szisz.

• The world's longest rally ever held covered a distance of 19,329 miles (31,107 km) from London, England, to Sydney, Australia. It took place between August and September 1977.

• The fastest speed achieved by a dragster over a 440-yard (400-meter) track is 316 mph (506 km/h). This was achieved in Topeka, Kansas.

• The winner of the most Formula One races is Frenchman Alain Prost. During his career he won 51 races. Argentinian driver Juan Fangio has won five drivers' championships — the most ever.

Racing words

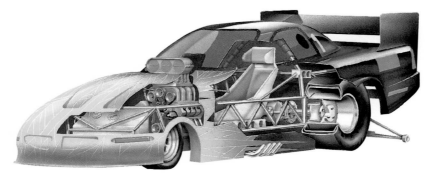

Cockpit
The part of a racing car where the driver sits. It contains the car's controls and the instruments that show how the car is performing.

Exhaust
A pipe, or number of pipes, that carry waste gases away from the engine.

Grid
The lineup of racing cars at the start of a race.

Pit area
The part of a racetrack where mechanics can work on a racing car during a race.

Safety cage
A cage of strong metal bars inside the racing car. This protects the driver in the event of a crash.

Skirting
The piece of body kit that runs around the base of a car.

Slick tire
A tire with no tread that is used in dry weather conditions.

Suspension
Systems of springs and pistons that absorb bumps on the road and stop the car from rocking around too much.

Index

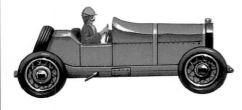

PHOTO CREDITS
Abbreviations: t-top, m-middle, b-bottom, r-right, l-left, c-center

Pages 4 & 7 – Hulton Getty Collection. 9, 10b, 12, 14b, 17t & b, 20t, 21b, 24 both, 25, 26 & 29 – Frank Spooner Pictures. 10t, 11b, 14-15, 15b & 17m – Empics. 11t, 20b, 21t, 24-25 & 28 both – Rex Features. 15t – Renault UK. 18 – Ford UK. 22 – Neil Smith.